# KING'S CROSS
## a tour in time

Mark Aston and
Lesley Marshall

First published by Camden Local Studies
and Archives Centre 2006
©London Borough of Camden

Camden Local Studies and Archives Centre
Holborn Library
32-38 Theobalds Road
London WC1X 8PA

www.camden.gov.uk/localstudies

ISBN: 1 900846 18 7

**Front cover illustration:**
View of Euston Road looking west
from Pentonville Road, c.1910

**Back cover illustration:**
Thirsty work! The Lucas Arms' darts
team, Gray's Inn Road, late-1940s

CRAS

WHIT

The Bruel

The

New Smallpox Hospital

Turnpike

to Islington

Pen

Paddington

Turnpike

From

Battle Bridge

Bowling
Green Hou:

The Pinde of Bedford

CONDUIT

Bagnige

Burying
Ground

St An
Ho

Hospital

FIELDS

Foundling

# Introduction

The locality covered by this book is quite small but it has a rich and varied history. The story begins with the Fleet River and a small settlement, which grew up at a place known as Battle Bridge, near the northern end of present-day Gray's Inn Road. Some of the earliest enterprises in the area were the spas, which developed around its springs, becoming fashionable resorts in the eighteenth century. It was, however, an early attempt at traffic planning which sealed the area's fate. In 1756 the New Road was cut across the fields from east to west to channel traffic away from the city centre. Today, as the ever-busy Euston Road, it serves the same purpose.

By the early nineteenth century Battle Bridge had become a depressing place. It was low lying and subject to flooding. The Smallpox Hospital had been built in 1769 and a fever hospital was added in 1802. It had become notorious for its tile kilns, rubbish tips and noxious trades. The Regent's Canal, opened in 1820, attracted other industries such as gas works.

A rescue attempt was made in 1829. How different it could have been if the Panarmonion project, offering recreational and cultural activities, had been a success. Its failure led to the site being developed for housing, leaving only Argyle Square as open space. Associated with the plan was a statue of King George IV built in the middle of the road junction. It gave the area a new name – King's Cross.

To most people the area is synonymous with the station. The arrival of King's Cross Station in 1852 followed by St Pancras in 1868 had an enormous impact, establishing it as an entry point to London for visitors, immigrants and goods from the North. The construction of the Underground lines confirmed it as a major interchange. For the people who lived in King's Cross these developments were a mixed blessing, providing work but also great upheaval. The expansion of land taken for railway use involved the demolition of whole streets of what were generally considered as slums, but many lost their homes and this added to overcrowding in the small terraced houses to the south of Euston Road. Model housing blocks such as Stanley Buildings, Derby Buildings, the late- Victorian flats of the Hillview Estate and more recent Council flats are examples of projects to provide the district with good, affordable housing.

Once the fortunes of King's Cross were linked to that of the railway industry, it also suffered from its problems. After surviving Second World War bombing the railways succumbed to post–war decline, particularly in goods traffic. Vast areas of sidings and warehouses became redundant and turned to wasteland. A low point was reached in 1966 when a plan was put forward to amalgamate the two termini, which would have meant the demolition of St Pancras Station. Since then a number of redevelopment schemes have come to nothing.

King's Cross has suffered from years of neglect. It is noisy and chaotic yet visitors and residents look upon it with affection. It has some success stories. Camley Street Natural Park beside the Regent's Canal provides a welcome green refuge. Euston Road is home to Camden Town Hall, the administrative centre of the Borough, and opposite is the prestigious new British Library. Next door, St Pancras Chambers is being restored. Work is underway at St Pancras International Station. From 2007 Eurostar trains will provide a link with Europe and in 2012 there will be a shuttle link with the Olympic site at Stratford. Arguments are raging over how the 67 acres of disused goods yards should be developed but there is no doubt that this will once again bring enormous change to King's Cross. Are its best days yet to come?

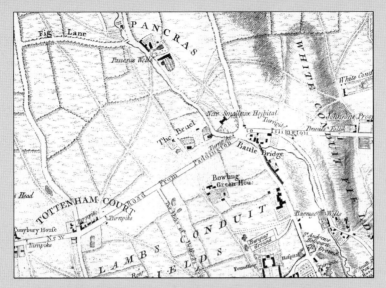

**1.** John Rocque's map of 1769 shows Battle Bridge crossing the Fleet River and the Smallpox Hospital beside the New Road (now Euston Road)

**2.** 'Near Battle Bridge, Middlesex', drawn and engraved by J J Smith and published in 1797

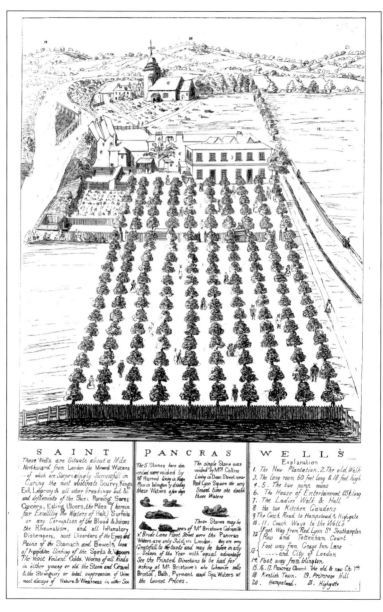

**3.** St Pancras Wells was one of a number of spas which flourished along the Fleet River. Situated to the south of St Pancras Church, it offered landscaped gardens and water with remarkable curative powers as can be seen in this eighteenth-century advertisement

**4.** Samuel Hieronymous Grimm sketched this in the 1770s, looking south along what is now Pancras Road, with St Pancras Church on the left. It is not quite an idyllic scene, as the buildings in the distance are the Smallpox Hospital and a tile kiln

*View of the inoculating Hospital at Pancras.*

**5.** Smallpox Hospital, 1806. Pioneering research was carried out here into the treatment and prevention of the disease. It was demolished in 1846 to make way for the building of King's Cross Station

**6.** Battle Bridge, 1814. The White Hart public house takes centre place in this deceptively quiet depiction of an area that grew into less than tranquil King's Cross. The location corresponds today to where Pentonville Road meets Gray's Inn Road. The Maidenhead public house, as denoted by its sign, was located on the corner of Maiden Lane (now York Way)

**7.** The Regent's Canal provided cheap transport for the tons of coal needed by the Imperial Gas Works which, when opened in 1824, was claimed to be the largest and finest in the world

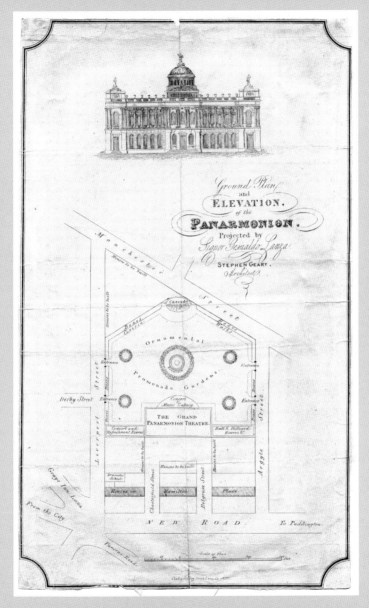

**8.** Plan of the Royal Panarmonion, c.1829, showing the proposed 'leisure centre' and park to the south of New (now Euston) Road with entrances in Argyle Street and Liverpool (now Birkenhead) Street. It was only partially completed

## ROYAL PANARMONION GARDENS,
### LIVERPOOL STREET, KING'S CROSS,
### NEW ROAD, St. PANCRAS.

## WILLIAM THE FOURTH
# Royal Car,
### STARTS ON THE
## SUSPENSION RAIL-WAY,
### EVERY MORNING AT 11 o'CLOCK,
#### AND CONTINUES
## RUNNING DURING THE DAY AT THE ABOVE GARDENS.

This astonishing Machine, now exhibiting in the Royal Panarmonion Gardens, is perhaps one of the most simple pieces of Machinery ever discovered, possessing such wonderful action, that many tons weight may be conveyed to any distance without the help of steam, or animal power. No one can believe that this Car travels with such ease and rapidity without being a witness of the fact. The idea is a very ingenious one, and does great credit to Mr. H. THOR-RINGTON, who is the inventor.

### *Refreshments may be obtained in the Gardens.*

Admittance One Shilling each Person, entitling the Party to a ride round the Gardens in the Royal Car, or on the Hobby Horse.
#### *ON SUNDAY, 6d. EACH PERSON TO WALK IN THE GARDENS.*

Johnson, Printer, 10, Brook Street, Holborn

**9.** Suspension Railway, c.1830.
A ride on this ingenious mode of transport was included
in the entrance fee to the gardens, which closed in 1832

**10.** King's Cross, by G S Shepherd, 1835.
A brief moment of glory for the monument that gave the area its name.
It was demolished ten years later

**11.** King's Cross Station, 23 October 1852. Depicted here just a week after its opening, the Lewis Cubitt designed building for the Great Northern Railway has since become London's oldest surviving railway terminus. Its 120 ft high clock tower remains a familiar landmark

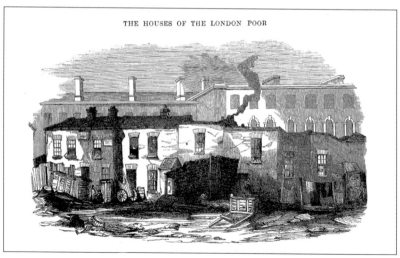

THE HOUSES OF THE LONDON POOR

**12.** In 1853 these homes beside the newly-built King's Cross Station were described as wholly unsafe for habitation, surrounded by filth and a source of disease. Blocks of flats such as nearby Stanley Buildings were intended to provide improved conditions

**13.** King's Cross Station, 1903. The station's early covered frontage, as seen here, was a lightweight structure with a glazed roof supported on cast iron columns. This was replaced during the 1970s by the green-edged canopy familiar to modern travellers. However, this too will soon be dismantled as part of the forthcoming re-landscaping of the station entrance

**14.** Lady passengers bringing Edwardian elegance to Victorian King's Cross Station, c.1904

**15.** King's Cross Station, 1905, showing the forecourt prior to the opening of the Piccadilly Line a year later

**16.** The Great Northern Hotel, King's Cross, c.1923. Designed by King's Cross Station architect Lewis Cubitt, the hotel opened on 17 May 1854. The building closed to guests in 2001; its future remains uncertain

**17.** Euston Road and King's Cross Station looking east from Belgrove Street, 8 July 1947. The building to the front right of the station is the street entrance to King's Cross Piccadilly Line; it was demolished in 1963

**18.** King's Cross Station, 1959. Overlooked by the 1956 Cinerama documentary *Seven Wonders of the World*, in which the presenter invites the audience to try and update the ancient list of wonders. The waiting passengers probably wouldn't include the train terminus amongst potential candidates!

**19.** The eternally busy junction between Euston Road, Pentonville Road and Gray's Inn Road, 1903. The arched sign to the right belonged to Reggiori's Restaurant

**20.** Reggiori's Swiss-Italian restaurant, shown here in 1897, served high-quality food and wine in opulent surroundings

**21.** The number 513 trolley bus on its way from
Parliament Hill Fields to Holborn Circus c.1960.
Note the two-way traffic in this section of Gray's Inn Road

**22.** Junction of Euston
Road and Gray's Inn Road,
c.1963. The stone in the
foreground marked the
boundary between the
former parishes of St
Pancras and Islington and
has stood on this site for
over two hundred years

**23.** The 'Lighthouse', 1978 – a King's Cross landmark
whose origin is a mystery

**24.** Seen here around 1971, King's Cross Cinema was completed in 1914 but its opening was delayed until 1920 due to First World War restrictions. Closing in 1993 as the Scala Cinema, the building is now a multi-purpose music venue

**25.** Constructing the Metropolitan Railway at King's Cross, 1861, showing the 'cut-and-cover' method of tunnelling. Pentonville Road can be seen to the right of the picture

**26.** King's Cross Metropolitan Railway Station, 1868. As the world's first urban underground railway, the Met. opened to public traffic on 10 January 1863 carrying some 40,000 passengers on this day

**27.** King's Cross Metropolitan Railway Station entrance,
Pentonville Road, c.1898; it closed a little over a decade later.
A rail connection still remains, as part of the King's Cross
Thameslink Station currently occupies the site

**28.** King's Cross Metropolitan Railway Station entrance,
King's Cross Bridge, 1933. It replaced the earlier entrance in nearby
Pentonville Road (see picture 27) until 1940 when it closed.
The building still remains today but minus its canopy

SIX DOORS FROM THE NEW METROPOLITAN RAILWAY STATION

**29.** The Bell public house, Pentonville Road, c.1863.
The pub undoubtedly 'rang' in the good times with the coming of the
Metropolitan Railway; King's Cross Met. Station was located just
'six doors' away. The building can still be seen today

**30.** King's Cross Thameslink, Pentonville Road, 2006. This glass fronted
building opened in 1983 as King's Cross Midland City Station.
However, its days are numbered, as plans are afoot to relocate to
St Pancras Mainline Station in 2007. The building to the left of
the station is the former Bell public house

**31.** A glimpse down Gray's Inn Road in 1927 reveals
familiar buildings but much less traffic

**32.** King's Cross Travelodge,
2006. The statue of Mercury,
messenger of the gods, dates
from the first use of the building
as headquarters of the Willing
advertising and press agency

Kings Cross Road. W. C.

**33.** King's Cross Road looking north, c.1906. The Golden Lion public house at the junction with Britannia Street is still open for business but, sadly, without its 'King of the Jungle' overseeing the thoroughfare's comings-and-goings

**34.** Derby Lodge, Wicklow Street, 2006.
The distinctive design identifies this as 'model' housing built by the Improved Industrial Dwellings Company, 1867-8

HAIR CUT & BRUSHED **3d.** BY CAMP'S PATENT MACHINERY.

THE ONLY HOUSE IN THE NEIGHBOURHOOD.

## THE PATENT ROTARY HAIR BRUSH.

Mr. A. J. WILLIAMS begs to invite the attention of his Friends and the Public generally, to the newly invented **ROTARY MACHINE BRUSH**, which he has just erected in his spacious Hair Cutting Saloon. It is one of the very best of its kind, and insures perfect comfort and cleanliness, which are such important desiderata in the art of the *perruquier.*—Come and judge.

## WILLIAMS' RESTORATIVE HAIR WASH.

This is an entirely **NEW MEDICATED HAIR CLEANSER** and **PURIFIER**, which will be found at once refreshing and invigorating during the process of **SHAMPOOING**. The clumsy, disagreeable, and antiquated method of Washing the Head in Water is entirely obviated by this new Invention of Mr. WILLIAMS.

## WILLIAMS' TRICHALLASMATIST.

This is one of the most surprising discoveries of the time. After much patient labour and research, Mr. W. has succeeded in producing a liquid of marvellous efficacy in restoring the Human Hair to its original hue. Mr. W. guarantees that while his **TRICHALLASMATIST** will effect a complete metamorphosis in the colour of the Hair to a Natural Brown or Black, not the smallest trace of the pigment will be discovered on the surface of the scalp. One of the valuable properties of this chromatic is, that it will effect the transformation gradually at the option of the person applying it. Experience is better than precept. Come, try, and be convinced.—TESTIMONIALS can be seen at the Establishment.

In Bottles, 7s. 6d., 15s., and £1. 1s.

Inventor and Proprietor of the

## TRICHOTROPHY, OR HAIR REGENERATOR.

*Sold in Bottles,* 2s. 6d., 5s. 6d., and 11s.

Gentlemen's Hair Cut on the most Improved principle, 3d.
Shampooing, 4d. Cut and Shampooed (at the same time) 6d. Curling, 3d.
Ladies' Hair Cut, 6d. Shampooed, 1s. Dressed, 6d.
*Clean Brushes used to each Person.—Ladies and Gentlemen waited on at their own Residences.*

SURGICAL INSTRUMENTS, and every description of CUTLERY, Ground, Set, and Repaired, on entirely new principles.

PLEASE NOTE THE ADDRESS:—

## A. J. WILLIAMS, 121, KING'S CROSS ROAD.

M. Bowry & Son, Printers, 46, King's Cross Road.

**35 & 36.** 'Hair today, gone tomorrow'. Advertisement for Andrew Williams' amazing hair restorative equipment and cures that were on offer at his premises at 121 King's Cross Road, c.1865. Today the building offers toppings of a different sort; 'It's Pizza Time', a takeaway food establishment, now occupies Mr Williams' former hair cutting saloon

**37.** Whitbread's bottled beer store, 1900. This is the Gray's Inn Road entrance to a large building which has had many uses. It was built in the 1820s as a horse and carriage repository and in 1834 housed Madame Tussaud's Waxworks Exhibition. It is now a car-servicing depot

**38.** Central London Throat and Ear Hospital, Gray's Inn Road, mid-1870s. The building opened in 1874 and is now the Royal Throat, Nose and Ear Hospital. St Jude's Church (1862-1936) can be partially seen to the left of the picture

**39.** Water Rats Theatre Bar, Gray's Inn Road, 2006. Formerly known as the Pindar of Wakefield public house, this has been the headquarters of the Grand Order of the Water Rats since 1986. Members of this charity must be associated with the entertainment profession and their leader is known as King Rat

**40.** Actor Bernard Bresslaw, King Rat in 1988, photographed with 'Coster Joe'

**41.** Baden-Powell hats and patriotism are displayed by the King's Cross Wesleyan Church Boy Scouts, c.1923

**42.** A class photograph was a serious matter for the pupils of Manchester Street School (now Argyle Primary School) in about 1927

**43.** Argyle Square, 2006. Small hotels have been in evidence in the square for the past hundred years and business is still flourishing, as these establishments on its eastern side demonstrate

**44.** Redding's cycle shop, 98 Cromer Street, 1912 on the corner with Whidborne Street. The Cromer Street Halal Grocer store now stands on the site

**45.** A fine balance! These smartly dressed 'likely' lads are posing outside Johnson's butchers shop at 6 Whidborne Street during the early-1950s

**46.** Fun in Midhope Street in the 1990s. The Hillview Festival has been held on the estate since 1981

**47.** Ladies day out. Posing for a picture outside the
Duke of Wellington public house (now McGlynn's pub),
5 Whidborne Street, during the late-1940s, these local ladies
were about to depart for their annual 'beano' to Southend-on-Sea

**48.** McGlynn's
public house, 2006.
This cosy looking
hostelry changed
its name from the
Duke of Wellington
ten years earlier

**49.** Number 6 Thanet Street, 1903. At the time of the 1901 census this was home to six families; a total of twenty three people in nine rooms. Poor but respectable, the men's occupations included omnibus and cab drivers, a printer, a photographer and a lamp lighter

**50.** Hastings Street looking west from Judd Street, c.1906. Today, Kelvin House, a British Telecom owned building dating back to the 1930s, can be found on the site of Dodd's Drug Store at 123 Judd Street

**51.** The Skinners Arms, 114 Judd Street, 1903. The youngsters are probably waiting for their fathers to finish 'refreshing' themselves inside. Meanwhile, the poster placed in the pub's window advertises the 1903 Football Cup Final between Bury and Derby County, later won convincingly by the Lancashire club 6-0!

**52.** Judd Street looking north towards Euston Road, c.1949.
The street was one of a number of temporary locations in the area
for the rather 'nomadic' King's Cross Coach Station (right).
The site is now occupied by Bramber flats and Judd Street Open Space

**53.** Voile and Wortley's liquorice factory, Bidborough Street, undated.
The stone horse on the roof is in the courtyard of Bidborough House,
which now stands on the site

**54.** The original terraced houses along Euston Road were set back from the carriageway. Over the years this space has gradually been built on but in 1903 numbers 13, 15 and 17 still retained their front gardens. Belgrove House now stands on this site between Crestfield Street and Belgrove Street

**55.** Euston Road, c.1960, with Belgrove House in the background on the right. Built in the 1930s, the frontage is shared at present by a post office and a burger restaurant

BRITISH COLLEGE OF HEALTH,
EUSTON ROAD, LONDON,
WHERE ALONE MORISON'S VEGETABLE UNIVERSAL MEDICINES ARE COMPOUNDED.

**56.** Miracle cure or quack medicine? James Morison's grand headquarters, built in 1828, on the corner with Argyle Street, gave a distinguished air to Euston Road. The building was replaced in 1900 by the Euston Palace of Varieties

**57.** The Regent Theatre, 37-43 Euston Road, 1924.
It began life as the Euston Palace of Varieties in 1900, changing its name to The Regent during the early-1920s. After a long spell as a cinema, and then a bingo hall, the building was eventually demolished to make way for the extension to Camden Town Hall which opened in 1977

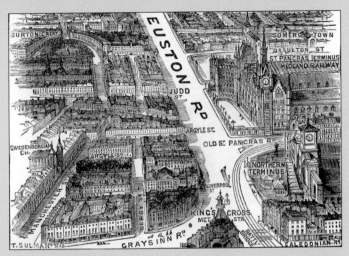

**58.** Bird's-eye view of Euston Road looking west from King's Cross, 1885.
Manchester Street later became Argyle Street and
Liverpool Street is now Birkenhead Street

**59.** Strenuous efforts by St Pancras Council on behalf of local residents
failed to prevent this vacant plot being used as a funfair in 1931.
The following year the Council had the final say when it bought
the land as the site for the new town hall

**60.** St Pancras Town Hall, now Camden Town Hall, was completed in 1937 and is seen here decorated for the Coronation of 1953

**61.** "The next jet leaving King's Cross St Pancras is non-stop to Manhattan." On 4 May 1969, and witnessed by residents atop The Chenies flats, Somers Town, Squadron Leader Tom Lecky-Thompson and his Harrier jump jet prepare to take part in the Daily Mail Transatlantic Air Race. This disused coal depot in Pancras Road (now Cooper's Lane Estate) provided the starting point

**62.** The Midland Railway Goods Depot, Euston Road, 1974.
The depot officially opened on 1 November 1887, the building of which
led to the controversial displacement of thousands of residents

**63.** The British Library, Euston Road, 2006. Designed by
Sir Colin St John Wilson and built on the site of the former
Midland Railway Goods Depot, the library was opened by the Queen in
1998. The building's brick and slate were chosen to harmonize with its
neighbour St Pancras Chambers (formerly the Midland Grand Hotel)

**64.** St Pancras Station trainshed as published in the *Building News* dated 26 March 1869. Opening for passenger traffic on 1 October 1868, it was designed by W H Barlow, the Midland Railway's chief engineer. At the time, its single span roof of 240 ft was wider than any other existing trainshed

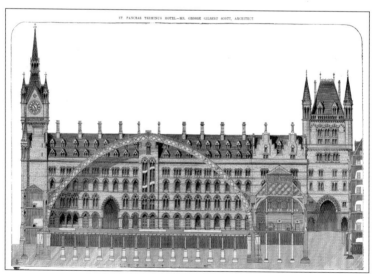

**65.** A rear view of the Midland Grand Hotel as published in the *Building News* dated 12 February 1869. A triumph of Victorian Gothic architecture by George Gilbert Scott, it opened in 1873 to provide luxurious accommodation for railway travellers

**66.** On a sunny day in about 1904, passengers on the
open-top horse buses pass Reggiori's and the shop of
Albert Baker, 'the up-to-date tobacconist'

**67.** When this photograph was taken in 1909, there were still gardens in front
of the buildings on Euston Road and the Great Northern Hotel (far right)

**68.** The west wing of the Midland Grand Hotel was completed in 1876.
Above the main entrance there was a ladies sitting room with a terrace,
shown in this view of about 1906 covered with a striped awning

**69.** The hotel closed in 1935 and was converted into offices known as St Pancras Chambers. Recent restoration has uncovered the original sumptuous decoration photographed here in 1997

**70.** Calm before the storm.
Trams and buses in 1939 .

**71 & 72.** St Pancras Station after the air raid on 10 May 1941.
The area around St Pancras and King's Cross Stations was an obvious
target for enemy bombers. It was one of the major railway centres of
London, with an electricity generating station and gas-works close by

**73.** An unusual view of the roof and chimneys of
St Pancras Chambers, 1997. In the distance is the back
of the only statue on the building, depicting Britannia

**74.** In 1992 during refurbishment of the building,
the statue of Britannia was found to be unsafe and
was brought down to earth for restoration

ALL CHANGE

**75.** Aerial photograph looking south, 1985,
showing the gas-holders in situ and the site of the
British Library cleared in preparation for its construction

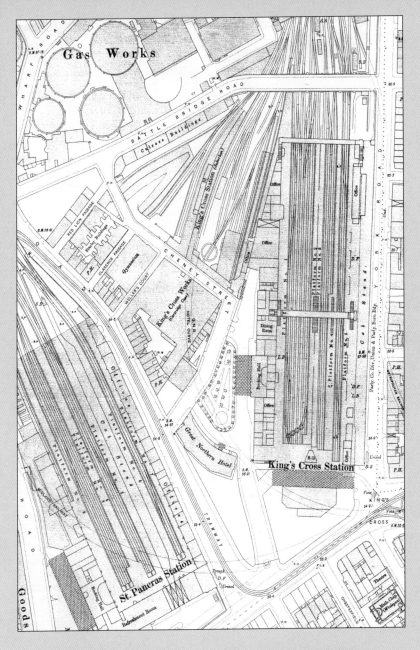

**76.** Ordnance Survey map, 1894-6, showing the buildings
between St Pancras and King's Cross Stations

**77.** Pancras Road, c.1904. All gone, including the Duke of Clarence public house (centre). The line of this road has been moved eastwards as part of the redevelopment of St Pancras Station

**78.** View of Stanley Buildings from Culross Buildings, late-1980s, showing the rear of the German Gymnasium to the left of the picture

**79.** The German Gymnasium, Pancras Road, as published in the
*Penny Illustrated Paper* dated 13 November 1869. The gym or 'Turnhalle'
was designed by Edward A Grüning and opened in January 1865 for the
German Gymnastic Society. It closed as a place of exercise in 1914,
after which it was bought by the Great Northern Railway

**80.** The Gymnasium, Pancras Road, 2006.
The newly refurbished former German Gymnasium now acts
as a prestigious information centre and exhibition space for the
St Pancras International Channel Tunnel Rail Link due to operate from 2007

**81.** Stanley Buildings, 1967. Completed in 1865 and named after Lord Stanley, chairman of the Improved Industrial Dwellings Company. Will the remaining two blocks survive?

**82.** Residents of Culross and Stanley Buildings on the roof of the latter, late-1980s

**83.** King's Cross Suburban Station sidings, 1980s. Added in 1924,
the 'island platform' was built on the site of the former engine stabling yard
to the west of the present suburban platforms. To the right of the picture is
Culross Buildings and to the left is the German Gymnasium, with
St Pancras Station trainshed looming behind

**84.** In 1992, the residents of Culross Buildings made their
feelings known regarding the lack of consultation about their future.
The fate of the block, dating from 1891-2, is still uncertain

**85.** Wasteland in the shadow of the gas-holders near Camley Street, 1981. The land was destined to be a lorry park until it was rescued by the London Wildlife Trust

**86.** Ken Livingstone, Greater London Council leader, officially opening the Camley Street Natural Park on 7 May 1985

**87.** The gas-holders across Regent's Canal, 1993
– more a work of art than industrial archaeology.
At present, all but one have been dismantled but
there are plans to incorporate some of them elsewhere
on the King's Cross Central redevelopment site

**88.** View across the redevelopment area from the roof of St Pancras Chambers, 1997

**89.** Work in progress, 2006 – photograph taken from Camden Town Hall

# Further Reading

*King's Cross: a tour in time* is not a complete history of King's Cross but a companion to the excellent books and articles listed below. These, as well as many more illustrations, are in the collections of the Camden Local Studies and Archives Centre, which you are welcome to come and view.

## Books

**Agar Town: the life and death of a Victorian "slum"**, by Steven Denford, 1995
**Change at King's Cross from 1800 to the present,**
by Michael Hunter and Robert Thorne, 1990
**East of Bloomsbury**, by David Hayes, 1998
**Holborn, Bloomsbury and Clerkenwell**, by Brian Girling, 1999
**Railways of Camden**, by Keith Scholey, 2002
**St Pancras Chambers formerly the Midland Grand Hotel,**
by London and Continental Stations and Property, 1996
**St Pancras Station**, by Jack Simmons; revised by Robert Thorne, 2003
**Streets of St Pancras, Somers Town and the Railway Lands,**
edited by Steven Denford and F Peter Woodford, 2002
**Survey of London vol. XXIV: King's Cross neighbourhood,**
by London County Council, 1952

## Articles

'A light at King's Cross: the 'Lighthouse' Building: fantasy and fact',
by David Hayes. **Camden History Review (CHR) 23**, 1999
'An amazing flow of spirits: the pleasure gardens of St Pancras',
by Rosemary Weinstein. **CHR 4**, 1976
'London's first northern by-pass: urban development and the New Road from
Paddington to Islington', by Catherine Durant. **CHR 15**, 1988
'Quackery at King's Cross: James Morison and the British College of Health',
by Shirley Neale. **CHR 28**, 2004
'The man who made King's Cross: the misfortunes of Stephen Geary',
by Robert Leon. **CHR 17**, 1992
'The romance of the Fleet River', by Richard Henwood. **CHR 11**, 1984
' "Without parallel in the known world": the chequered past of
277 Gray's Inn Road', by David Hayes. **CHR 25**, 2001

# Acknowledgements

The authors wish to thank all those who have made this publication possible, in particular our colleagues at Camden Local Studies and Archives Centre for their support and advice, and to Kareen Husbands and Ros Daniel of Camden Council's Design Team. A very special thanks to Leslie McCartney and Alan Dein of King's Cross Voices Oral History Project for their kindness in locating images from their collection for reproduction in this book.

The following have kindly given their permission to reproduce illustrations:

Thelma Dowsett/King's Cross Voices, 45, back cover
Aidan Flood, 88
Brian Girling, 33, 50
Guildhall Library, City of London, 10
Hawker Siddeley/Tom Lecky-Thompson, 61
London Metropolitan Archives, City of London, 23
London's Transport Museum © Transport for London, 17, 26, 28
Alban Lote/King's Cross Voices, 44, 47
Jessie McKenzie/King's Cross Voices, 42
Museum of London/The Henry Grant Collection, 81
National Museum of Science and Industry, 18
Steve Neylon, 83
Catherine Packard/King's Cross Voices, 46
Karel Schwartz/Battlebridge Residents Association, 78, 82
Alec/Mimi Wallis, 84

All other illustrations have been supplied by the authors and Camden Local Studies and Archives Centre. Every attempt has been made to trace copyright holders. Apologies in advance to those concerned if an oversight has occurred: corrections will be included in any future editions of this publication.